What is an Earthquake?

By Elizabeth Drummond

Library For All Ltd.

LIBRARY
FOR ALL
DIGITAL LIBRARY
FOR THE WORLD

Library For All is an Australian not for profit organisation with a mission to make knowledge accessible to all via an innovative digital library solution. Visit us at libraryforall.org

What is an Earthquake?

First published 2021

Published by Library For All Ltd
Email: info@libraryforall.org
URL: libraryforall.org

This book was made possible by the generous support of the Education Cooperation Program and the following organisations.

Australian Aid

ChildFund Australia

PLAN INTERNATIONAL

AHP Disaster READY

What is an Earthquake?
Drummond, Elizabeth
ISBN: 978-1-922550-15-6
SKU01565

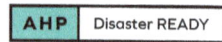

What is an Earthquake?

Tectonic plates

This is the Earth.

Look closely and you will see that the Earth's surface is not a single piece of land, but lots of smaller pieces called tectonic plates. These plates fit together like a jigsaw puzzle.

Tectonic plates move all the time. Some are under the land, while some are under the sea. They usually move so slowly that you won't feel anything at all.

Did you know?

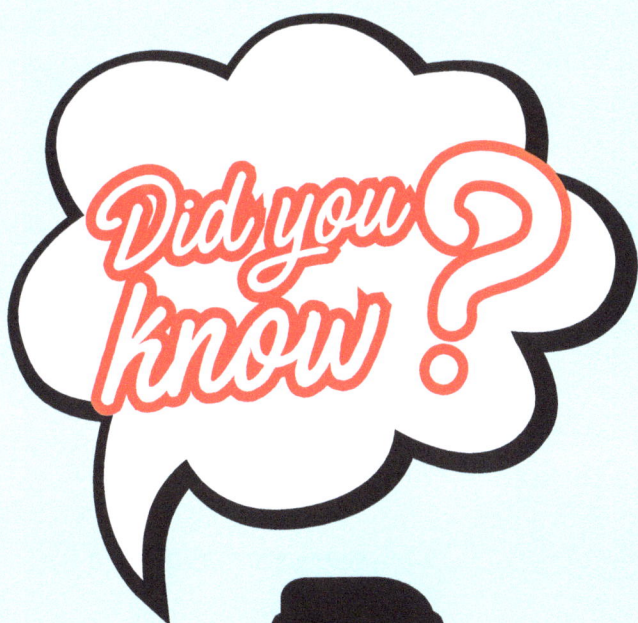

Tectonic plates usually move about 2–5cm a year. That's about as fast as your fingernails grow!

Earthquakes

Sometimes tectonic plates move very quickly.

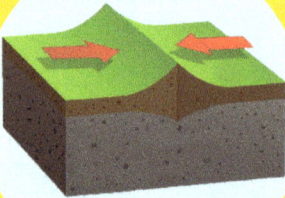

They can bump hard into each other.

They can slide and grind past each other.

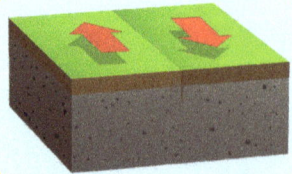

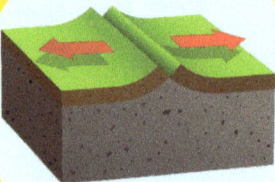

They can even pull apart.

Q&A

[Question]
What do you think happens when tectonic plates bump, grind or drift apart?

[Answer]
The ground shakes and it is called an earthquake!

What happens when the ground shakes?

Earthquakes can be very small. When this happens, the ground only shakes a little bit. A small earthquake can feel like a big truck just drove by. Lights can swing, things might fall off a shelf, or trees might sway.

Earthquakes can be big! A big earthquake can cause the ground to shake so much that it will crumble and crack. Some houses may shake until they fall down.

A big earthquake can be very dangerous as you could be hurt by falling objects.

Earthquakes make new land

Earthquakes can be very destructive, but they can also make new land.

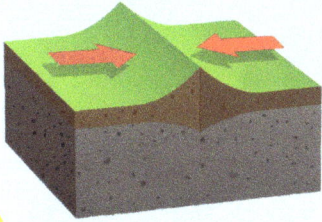

When tectonic plates bump into each other they can form new mountains.

When tectonic plates drift apart they can form a new piece of ocean floor.

Tsunamis

Sometimes earthquakes happen under the ocean. This shaking can cause waves to form. As these waves roll closer to land, they get bigger, and bigger, and bigger!

These big waves are called tsunamis.

Tsunamis are very dangerous as the fast moving water can rush into buildings and wash away cars or people.

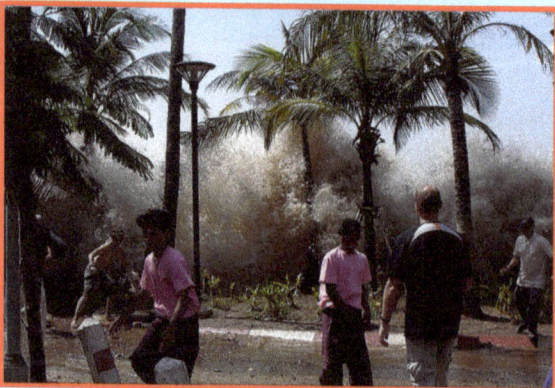

Landslides

Sometimes an earthquake will shake a mountain or steep ground. This shaking can cause the surface to come loose and fall down the mountain like a river of dirt, rocks and vegetation. This is called a landslide.

Stay safe inside during an earthquake

If you feel the ground start to shake then DROP, HIDE and HOLD ON!

1

Try to move outside. If it is not safe to do so, then drop to the floor.

2

Hide under your house, or under a table, where nothing can hit you.

3

Hold on tight to something that won't move, like a strong table or steps.

17

Stay safe outside during an earthquake

Some places are safer than others if you are outside during an earthquake.

1

Move away from trees or buildings that can fall on you.

2

Find a flat area away from hills in case the earth starts to slide.

3

Run away from the beach to high ground in case a tsunami is triggered.

4

If you are in a car then pull over and stop, but stay inside the car as it can protect you from falling objects.

More earthquake safety!

1

Talk to your community about earthquakes and make a community action plan.

2

After the earthquake has stopped go to the safe place you have identified with your community.

3

Don't go inside a building after an earthquake until an adult has told you it is safe.

Stay safe!

Pretend you can feel the ground suddenly start to shake.

What will you do? Look around you. Can you see somewhere safe? Quickly move into this safe place.

Practise moving to safe places inside and outside.

Let's play a game!

Mark each square when you have completed the activity!

Read an information book about earthquakes.	If you need to leave your house in an emergency, where will you go? Ask your family or teacher about your community action plan!	
Tell someone three facts you've learned about earthquakes.		Do you know what to do if you are inside during an earthquake?
	Make an earthquake action plan with your community.	Do you know what to do if you are outside during an earthquake?

Photo credits

Page	Link
Cover	https://pixabay.com/photos/earthquake-rubble-collapse-disaster-1665878/
Title Cover	https://pixabay.com/photos/earthquake-fracture-asphalt-split-1665892/
8 & 15	https://www.shutterstock.com/image-illustration/four-illustrations-different-types-plate-tectonics-753188128
10-11	https://pixabay.com/photos/lamp-lightbulb-electricity-old-1031516/ https://pixabay.com/photos/semi-trailers-truck-road-trailers-534577/ https://pixabay.com/illustrations/tree-oak-oak-tree-quercus-1544695/
12-13	https://pixabay.com/photos/earthquake-rubble-collapse-disaster-1665886/ https://commons.wikimedia.org/wlkl/Earthquake#/media/File:Chuetsu_earthquake-earthquake_liquefaction1.jpg https://commons.wikimedia.org/wiki/File:Shizuoka_earthquake_struck_room_20090811.jpg
16-17	https://pixabay.com/photos/tsunami-riptide-natural-disaster-67499/ https://pixabay.com/photos/giant-wave-curling-lighthouse-1156627/ https://pixabay.com/photos/landslide-landslip-erosion-road-2819155/

Emergency decision-making tree

Prior to the event of a tsunami, tropical cyclone, flooding, landslide or earthquake, speak with your family and teacher about your community's evacuation building or safe place.

Discuss how to respond to possible scenarios, and use the decision tree to help you decide the best course of action.

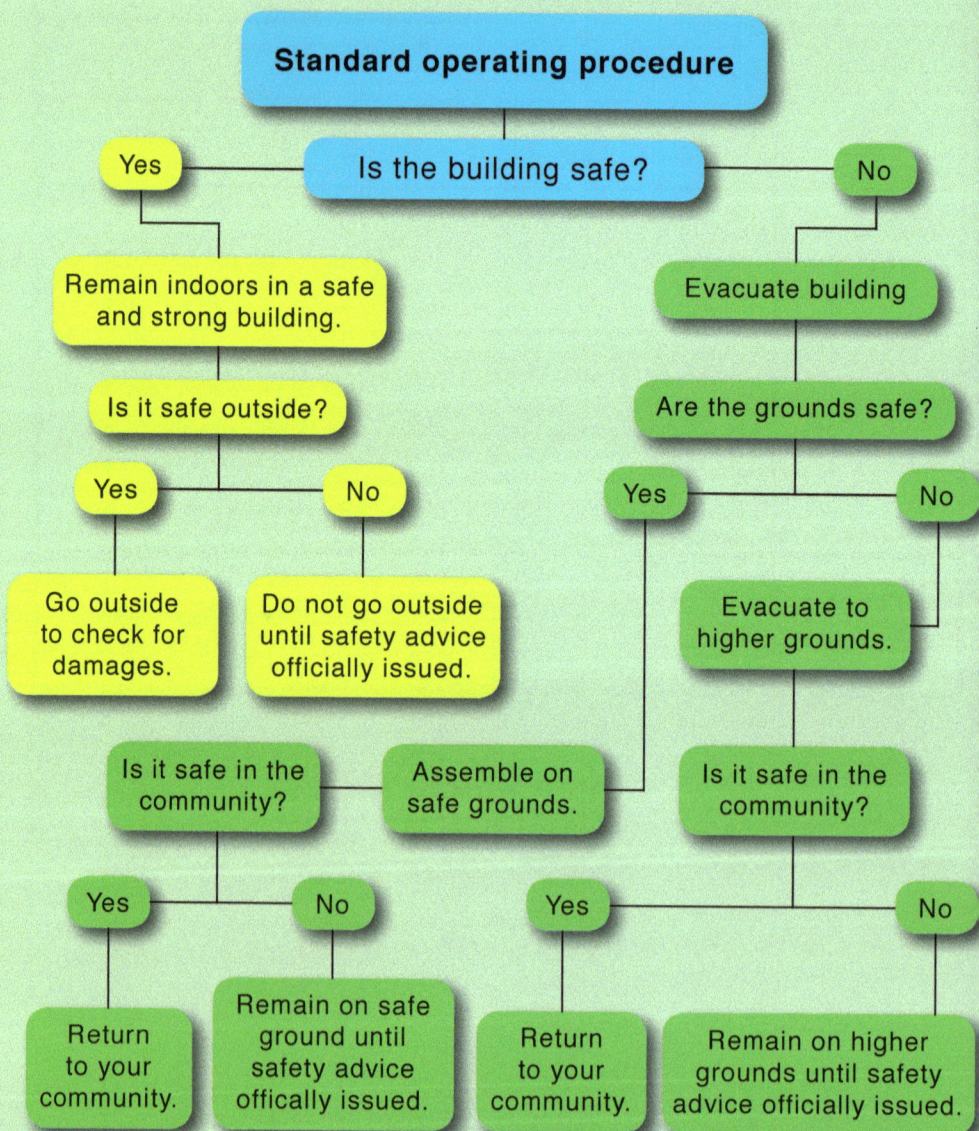

Standard operating procedure

Is the building safe?

Yes → Remain indoors in a safe and strong building.

No → Evacuate building

Is it safe outside?

Are the grounds safe?

Yes → Go outside to check for damages.

No → Do not go outside until safety advice officially issued.

Yes → Evacuate to higher grounds.

No → Evacuate to higher grounds.

Is it safe in the community?

Assemble on safe grounds.

Is it safe in the community?

Yes → Return to your community.

No → Remain on safe ground until safety advice offically issued.

Yes → Return to your community.

No → Remain on higher grounds until safety advice officially issued.

Supporting information

Emergency kit

Keep an emergency kit at home for your family.

The kit must contain:

First Aid Kit

Torch lamp

Radio

Batteries

Drinking water

Preserved food

Matches

Use the kit only in case of emergency and replace anything that has been used.

Shelter-in-place

Earthquake:

- Identify safe places where you can protect your head and avoid heavy falling objects.
- Don't forget an earthquake can cause a tsunami.
- If you feel a strong earthquake, go quickly to higher ground, and listen to the radio for warnings.

Tropical cyclone:

- Open louvers on the side of the building, away from wind to reduce the pull force of the wind on the roof.
- Remain calm, stay indoors but clear of doors and windows.
- Remain in the strongest part of the building.

Do not go outside until safety advice is officially issued.

Evacuate building

Assist people with disability and visitors.

Take your emergency kit.

Evacuate to higher ground and move to a safe location.

Tsunami:

- Run to a safe place in high ground or at least 2 km inside the island.
- Wait for at least 2–3 hours after the first wave to return to the village.

Listen to the radio for further information or reach out to the emergency contacts.

You can use these questions to talk about this book with your family, friends and teachers.

What did you learn from this book?

Describe this book in one word. Funny? Scary? Colourful? Interesting?

How did this book make you feel when you finished reading it?

What was your favourite part of this book?

About the contributors

Library For All works with authors and illustrators from around the world to develop diverse, relevant, high quality stories for young readers. Visit libraryforall.org for the latest news on writers' workshop events, submission guidelines and other creative opportunities.

Did you enjoy this book?

We have hundreds more expertly curated original stories to choose from.

We work in partnership with authors, educators, cultural advisors, governments and NGOs to bring the joy of reading to children everywhere.

Did you know?

We create global impact in these fields by embracing the United Nations Sustainable Development Goals.

libr/aryforall.org